T0354566

*Irene
and her
6<sup>th</sup> Sense*

# *Irene and her 6ᵗʰ Sense*

## *203*

### Rajith Rajappan

PARTRIDGE

A Penguin Random House Company

**To order additional copies of this book, contact**
Partridge India
000 800 10062 62
www.partridgepublishing.com/india
orders.india@partridgepublishing.com

# FOREWORD

I am thankful to Partridge Publishers for giving me an opportunity to bring out this book. Special thanks to Jireh Ingod, Geema Ramos, and the entire editing team at Partridge Publishing, who ensured that everything went smoothly.

It would be unfair If I don't give credit to my specially gifted friends—Karthik Abhirama Krishna (for designing the cover page and the back cover), Vishal Kant, Ashok Kolla, Reema Raghuraj, and Shwetambari M, who directly or indirectly pushed me to do something new always, and of course, my parents, who continue to tolerate my maverick ways of doing things.

And thanks to the readers for purchasing this book. I sincerely hope you will feel good from within once you reach the end of the book! God bless. Enjoy life!

# NOTE FROM THE AUTHOR

- **Iris Halmshaw**, a three-year-old with autism. She can't talk, but her beautiful paintings sell for hundreds: Iris Grace was diagnosed with autism in 2011. She struggles to interact with others or maintain eye contact, according to a website set up by her parents. As part of her therapy, Iris's parents encouraged her to take up painting, which she quickly grew to love, spending up to two hours on elaborate pieces.

Read more at http://www.huffingtonpost.com/2013/07/01/iris-halmshaw-paintings-autistic-thousands_n_3530466.html

- Seven-year-old **Kieron Williamson**'s paintings fetch £150,000: His mother, Michelle, said, 'Until last year, he didn't draw anything, and in fact, we had to draw dinosaurs for him to colour in. The turning point was when we took our first family holiday to Devon and Cornwall last May, and he liked the boats and scenery. He asked for some plain paper and started drawing his own stuff.'

Read more at http://www.dailymail.co.uk/news/article-1203226/Pictured-Incredible-watercolour-paintings-boy-aged-just-SIX.html

I sincerely believe if you really want to do something in this world, then be grateful for whatever talents you have and work hard at it. Don't worry about the age factor. There is no age limit in finding out what gifts you possess—sometimes it comes early in life and sometimes after going through lots of rough patches. Whatever may be the case, once you start recognising your talent (whether it is writing or painting or singing or dancing or selling or inventing or practicing mentalism or whatever), then work hard at it. Make the most of yourself.

# PART 1

PART 1

# CHAPTER 1

Sitting on the outside compound wall of the school, looking at the sky, Irene was about to cry. Gradually, tears began to roll down her cheeks. She had only one question to ask God—why me?

Irene was the only child of Isabella and Darius. Darius had come from a small town and settled in Bradley City. Initially, he used to do odd jobs to sustain his family. Later, whatever money he used to earn from these jobs, he would invest on upgrading his skills. He registered himself in one of the institutes to learn typing. There were many jobs as a typist in all sectors during the 1970s. As fate favoured, he landed a small-time job as typist in one of the educational institutes run by the government.

The following year, he married Isabella from his village and brought her to Bradley City and started to live in the quarters provided by the institute. The salary offered by the educational institute was less, but people liked working in the institutes run by the government because of the many perks they enjoyed. All people could avail housing facilities based on their grades and type of work. Only a nominal amount would be cut from the salary. They also had hospital services inside the institutes, and people who worked there could avail it free of cost. In other words, life became very comfortable once you got a job in the government-run institutes. You didn't have to worry about the outside world. It was a very secure life.

Two years after their marriage, Irene was born. As Irene was growing up, she realised that her life was not smooth. Her parents used to quarrel every day. Isabella came from a family that was relatively better compared to that of Darius. So she had higher expectations about their life, which Darius found hard to subscribe to. Subsequently, whenever relatives of either of the couple visited them, they would quarrel even in their presence. Their marital life had become a joke among the neighbours. Darius's squandering ways to get attention did not go well with Isabella.

When Irene started to realise the effect her parents' constant quarrelling was having on her, she began to spend most of her time after school in the library. A significant influence on Irene during her growing-up years was the spirit of competitiveness her mother inculcated in her. She wanted Irene to be first in the class. Her direction was clear: 'We are having a terrible financial condition. Dad is trying his best to take care of all, so if you don't study well, you will become one like us.' These emotional lessons that Isabella imparted in Irene made her to work harder.

When Irene was first admitted to school, she found a strange thing happening to her—she was not able to understand anything. All the subjects were going above her head except for drawing lessons. She used to enjoy painting and colours, but when it came to other subjects like mathematics, English, and so on, she was not able to read or comprehend anything. To read one sentence, she would take lots of time.

When she told this problem to her mother, Isabella shrugged it off as lazy attitude and enrolled her in a small-time coaching institute. Without understanding what Irene was undergoing, her mother used to again give her 'emotional medicines': 'See what kind of life we are leaving. Do you want to suffer like us? Do you know with how much difficulty we are sending you to school? And now we have additional expenditure in the form of your tuition. I will not tolerate this kind of lazy attitude.'

In the tuition centre, the same story continued. All others would solve the problems given to them with ease, while Irene would take lots of time. In the school, every month they had monthly exams. In one of the exams, Irene scored 'A+' in drawing and 'E' in other subjects. As per the school administration, students who fail to get passing mark should get signature from their parents on the assessment card for those subjects.

Irene was very happy to see her drawing score, but she was not sure how her parents would react after seeing the complete assessment card. She discarded any negative thoughts and headed home from school.

# CHAPTER 2

Irene was not aware of what was happening in the house. A few hours before she reached home, Darius and Isabella had a big fight. They were both still nursing their egos, but both pretended as if they are occupied in some work. Isabella entered her house, and in a very elated mood, threw her bags, took the score card, and handed it over to her mother, before she headed to the kitchen to get hold of something to eat. As she was about to put a pancake in her mouth, a tight slap singed her face. She was totally shocked. For a moment she felt as if her eardrum had burst. She was accustomed to only seeing her mother's angry mood and her angry eyes on her angry face. After a few seconds, when she got hold of her sense, Isabella got a cane from outside and started hitting Irene. She poured out on Irene all the anger she had as a result of the fight with Darius. In the end, she gave her the same emotional lecture she always gave Irene, and finally said, 'I don't know how you are going to do—but if you don't pass in all the subjects in the next month's test, we will stop sending you to school.'

Irene walked out of the house, gradually taking each step very fast. She was not sure where she was heading. Lots of thoughts were flowing in her mind. This was the first time she had seen her mother so angry. Her father had got up and tried to reach her, but by the time he could take control of the situation, Irene had already walked far way. Lost in thoughts, she reached the school compound wall and sat there for some time. She saw lots of vehicles passing by, children strolling with her parents in a jovial mood, leaves carried along by the breeze, birds chirping, and the sound of the slap which felt on her like a thunder. Lifting her eyes to the sky, as tears started to roll down her face, she asked God, 'Why me!'

# CHAPTER 3

As she was pondering about what to do next, she found two parrots sitting on the tree. Both were screaming, but she listened carefully and found that they were talking, as if imitating the sounds of each other. This act went on for many hours and an idea struck her mind. She ran to the library, picked the history textbook, read a few paragraphs in silence, and started repeating it again and again. The words started entering her mind. And after some fifty attempts, she found that she could rattle off the whole paragraph without looking at the textbook. She got the solution. Now this is what she was going to do—commit each theory subject to memory. Learning by heart entire chapters became her weapon. It would consume lots of time, but it made her pass her exams. But with mathematics, she found that this technique was not helping, so to tackle it, she started writing each problem many times till she got hold of those questions. And in the exams, she would solve those questions whose wordings were similar to what she had prepared.

In this way, she cleared all her exams, and in one of the final examinations, she came third in the school. Overjoyed by this, she felt a feeling of self-control. Now she no longer worried about examinations or feared beatings from her mother at home. The quarrelling between her parents, however, continued at home, but she would spend more time in the library and at her friend's place, learning subjects by heart. In the class, thanks to her strong ability to learn by heart, she impressed the teachers as they got word by word of what was written in the text books. Now Irene was among the brightest students in the class, among the top five, and Irene started enjoying this attention.

As she started moving to higher grades, she began to face problems. In the higher grade, application of subject knowledge was more important, and her skill to learn by heart was not helping her much. She managed to clear exams, but lack of understanding of topics made her one among the average scorers. She didn't bother as long as she was passing the exams. Time flew, and she reached the twelfth grade, her last at the institute.

The institute had provision for enrolling students from primary to higher secondary classes, that is, from first to twelfth grade. After that, if students wanted to pursue their education further, they had to sit for competitive exams to get admission to engineering or other professional courses. Irene was not sure what to do with her life. Her father had eight years left before he retired from the government institute as senior typist. Irene had made up her mind that before her father retired, she should at least have a professional degree that would help her land a job in a well-known firm.

With that in mind, she started appearing for competitive exams for admission to engineering courses. Initially, she did not find much success, but she kept appearing for exams of well-known institutes. In the Bradley City, there were lots of engineering institutes mushrooming. Getting into a government-run engineering institute required a high score, whereas in the private institutes, one could secure admission even with a low score, but the seats were under management quota. This meant that you had to shell out some 'add on' fees on top of the school feels.

So as not to be left behind in the rat race, Irene started appearing for exams of all the institutes, and she started getting calls from all the low-rung institutes. As expected, the fees under the management quota was huge. She wanted to discuss with her father to help her, but the financial condition in her house was not favourable, and she knew it would be turned down. She therefore decide to take a break for a year and focus on getting admission into top-rung government institutes where fees is less. And once she has ensured admission, she thought she could take her father's help to avail educational loan if required.

Her friends were all getting into well-known institutes. Every day when friends hung out, one or other would have a reason to celebrate for getting admission in an engineering institute. This pained Irene a lot, and she was ashamed of telling her plans to them. However, as time passed by, everyone went on as per their calling. That's when Irene realised the importance of understanding the concepts of a subject and learning to apply them rather than merely committing everything to memory. Had she not resorted to learning subjects by heart, she could have now made it to one of the top-rung institutes. She realised that just passing exams were her primary focus, while she made no attempts at understanding the nitty-gritty of the subjects. One can pass the subjects by mugging up, but in the long term, this strategy would not pay any dividends. In competitive exams, all top-rung institutes test the candidate's ability for application of subject knowledge. She decided to take a break and try to work on understanding the subjects at a deeper level. Hence she took a route different from that of her friends. Not joining any institute and working on her weakness became her motto—a road less travelled.

# CHAPTER 4

**B**uoyed by the newfound enthusiasm, Irene went to the library and gathered all the books necessary to make her prepare for the competitive examination. Her parents were a little worried by her strange decision, but they later gave in when her eagerness to join a good institute and make a good career became obvious.

She spent day and night delving into the depths of each subject. Sometimes an entire day would be spent to understand one topic. She did not bother initially as her goal was clear, but gradually, over a period of time, she felt her energy draining away and her enthusiasm weakening. She was putting more effort to grasp the subjects, but her mind was very slow. And when she thought she understood a concept very well and tried to solve the kind of problems that appear in competitive exams, she was not able to do it. Her fifteen years of learning concepts by heart was creating a hindrance. She was not able to switch to a new mode of understanding the concepts. She estimated that if it went like this, then even after a year, she would not be able to prepare herself fully. This was not going anywhere, she realised. She started getting mentally frustrated. She needed a break, she thought.

She got up from her study table, looked outside her window, and gazed at the sky. Far away, she saw a few children, five to seven-year-olds, going to a nearby tuition centre, carrying school bags. She felt nostalgic; she was also once sent to the tuition centre by her mother when she was not doing well at school. Immediately, an idea struck her—couldn't she be of help to these children? Teaching the junior grade lessons would not take much effort. Moreover, some of the 'learn by heart' skills and techniques that she herself had developed, which had proved very useful to her then, could be of use to these kids now.

With that aim in mind, she approached the head of the tuition centre and asked them if they needed a part-time tutor for their learning centre. She told them of her credentials and also agreed to do this work at half the amount usually paid to other tutors. From the following week, she started teaching students. She felt at peace with herself. Besides, it was a nice break from the mental effort required to understand the subjects for competitive exams.

By the month end, she received her first pay. The amount was sufficient to take care of her daily needs. She didn't have to ask for money from her parents now. She bought some exquisite eatables from her first pay and gave a treat to her parents. She wanted to give a party to her friends also, but now most of them did not find time for her as they were very busy with their studies. Getting admission was hard enough, but once admitted, clearing the exams to get the engineering degree was even harder—Irene knew this, and this idea did not go well with her way of life. She liked freedom. She was now having much more time. No one could understand the immense peace and joy she was undergoing now. She cut down on the time for her friends and started to juggle her time between her studies and giving tuitions.

After few months, when she had saved sufficient amount of money, she felt an urge to travel, to see different places and people and their culture. So she got the tour map and started searching for a place to visit. It should not be far away from Bradley, should be within her budget, and also allow her to spend more time with nature. She zeroed in on twelve to thirteen places which would be visited on every weekend. Her plan was simple—Monday to Friday, studying for exams and give tuitions. On Friday evening, she would head towards her targeted place via rail or bus, and on Sunday evening, she would return.

The prospect of spending her weekends travelling made her more enthusiastic towards her studies. She began to focus better gradually, and she was doing much better in understanding concepts than before. Being a girl and travelling alone on weekends was a risky proposition, but she wanted to give it a try. Anyway, she had taken a different path compared to her friends— so why not try this also? She followed her gut feeling and stuck to her plans for the following three months. On a few trips, she often took her mother also along. They both were mesmerised with nature's beauty. Until then their lives were confined to the institute campus and they hardly went outside. This change was refreshing, and Irene's mind started becoming more free and started appreciating nature's beauty.

In one of the trips, she went trekking with a few people. It was so tiring that when she came back, she felt like giving up everything and just lie down. And she did just that. After reaching her house on Sunday at 4 p.m., she ate a little, got fresh, and lay down on the bed. When her eyes opened, it was 5 a.m. the following day. But she was feeling something strange. Her head was feeling heavy; she wanted to download whatever was there in her head onto a paper. She got up, went to her study table, took out a blank sheet and pencil, and started sketching. Whatever picture came to her mind, she transferred it onto the paper. After two hours of sketching, when the work was done, she was amazed by the final product. The sketch represented the landscape of the places she visited. It had come out very well, and she enjoyed it. It was a free-flow sketch done without any effort. She sat with the sketch in her hand and kept gazing at it for a few minutes.

Tears started flowing down her cheeks. She realised what she had missed for so many years. She was born to paint and she never realized it. When she was small, she used to like paintings, but she succumbed to the pressures of family and society and ended up doing things she did not like. And now she was sitting with one of her masterpieces. Life was not unfair. All the incidents which happen have a hidden meaning. Thanks to her tendency to learn everything by heart, she developed a good memory and an ability to store information. And now it became useful. And listening to her gut feelings and travelling on every weekend to be with nature helped her mind to capture beautiful landscapes. And when the time came to release it, the sleep caused by the stress during trekking helped the mind to arrange everything—and now the product was in her hand.

Now she was able to think clearly. It was not engineering she wanted to do but painting, and she would further pursue to hone her skills. This time she did not feel like asking her friends or relatives. Her best friend was her gut–feeling or intuition. Within a few weeks from this incident, Irene enrolled herself in the Bradley School of Arts.

# CHAPTER 5

Bradley School of Arts was unique in its own way. It always attracted people from diverse backgrounds. And it was also one of the affordable schools. Irene paid only one-fourth of the amount her friends paid as tuition. Her father was able to pay the amount from his savings.

It was day one at the institute, and all were expected to be there by 8 a.m. The first lecture was supposed to be delivered by the dean of the institute. Irene, with her recharged attitude, thought of reaching the place half an hour before the scheduled time so that she could explore the inside of the school. She was expecting a big classroom, but she was shocked to know that the lectures were usually held outside, in the midst of nature.

There were approximately twenty people enrolled for the one-year course. The one-year course is bifurcated into six months of experiential learning and six months of internship. In the first six months, students would be assigned one mentor each under whom they would learn the basics of paintings. In the next six months, to graduate as a professional artist, they would be doing apprenticeship sponsored by the corporates.

At 8 a.m., near a sculpture in an open space surrounded by greenery, every one gathered. The sculpture was drawing lots of attention, and when the dean arrived to give his lecture, he started by talking about why that sculpture had been stationed there. That sculpture was created by passing-out students. Every year as per institute protocol, the passing-out students have to come up with something new, as a token of reminder of what they have learnt. He kept his speech short and told the students that his only expectation from the students is that 'when you pass out, you should grow from within. When you have grown from within, you would be able to attract favourable situations as per your needs, and at that point, you will realise your natural potential. And arts help you achieve that.' There was a deafening applause for the dean's motivational speech.

Irene was hooked to the dean's speech, but half her attention was also on a guy standing some distance away from her, listening to the speech. His build and looks mesmerised Irene. She felt like sketching him naked. She woke up from her imagination as the students started greeting each other. When he introduced himself to other students, Irene came to know that Victor was his name. Irene wanted to know more about him, but she thought instead of hurrying up, she would take this forward step by step. In the initial few months, everyone was busy with their assigned mentors. The day used to be hectic. After attending the morning lectures every day, they would be given some assignments. The assignments were mainly on teaching students how to capture nature's beauty on the drawing board.

Irene was pretty good at that as she had learned a lot during her weekend travels that she did while studying for competitive exams. So she enjoyed her assignments with gusto, and one of her sketches was also displayed on the notice board to be seen by others. She was gradually becoming popular, but she was not getting the attention of the one person she was craving for. It was during one of the breaks that Irene mustered up the courage to approach Victor and tell him, 'Hi Victor, my roommate, Pepper, has asked me to pass on a message to you. She feels for you and would like to go for a date with you. She wanted to tell you all this personally but did not gather strength, hence requested my help.'

Victor felt amazed and did not know what to respond; he just smiled and went back to the classroom. The next day, he saw Irene standing outside the cafeteria and asked her, 'How is your roommate, Pepper? I was thinking about her date offer the whole night, and I have taken a decision that instead of going with your roommate, I would like to call you for a date.'

Irene wanted to tell him yes immediately but did not want to show him she was desperate. She was shivering at the thought of going with a date with Victor, but she controlled herself and pretended that she did not listen to anything and moved away. As the days passed by, Victor kept approaching her and Irene kept avoiding him. In the meanwhile, Victor started getting lots of proposal from other girls, asking him for a date. Victor was not a flirt, but he now started enjoying the attention he was getting. He accepted a few of them, and the day he went out for a date, that became the main topic of discussion among girls in the hostel that night. Going for a date with Victor had now become a hot topic in the girls' hostel.

When the news of his dates reached Irene, she would shrug it off, stating, 'Thank god, I did not go for a date. I pity girls who are getting used by him. I don't feel like being called "one of Victor's girls".'

There were many instances where Victor and Irene had to come together and finish the task given by their mentors. Where work was concerned, Victor was very professional, and Irene respected him for that. Gradually, they became good friends.

# CHAPTER 6

The time for apprenticeship had come. The students were grouped into separate teams and the list of teams was put up on the noticeboard. Irene felt a sharp pinch in her heart when she saw that Victor was teamed up with another student. That was when for the first time Victor engendered some special feelings in Irene. Anyway, she thought the feeling would fade away by the evening.

But every day, the same feelings reappeared. Not able to concentrate on work, she decided to give him a call. She called up Victor and asked him to come to a nearby museum. After discussing the usual arts-related topics, she asked him a personal question. She wanted to know if he had someone who he cared for. Victor felt a little awkward, but he just smiled and left it.

As the days passed, they started meeting every weekend. Irene started liking him a lot. His face, his smell, and his cool attitude caused in her an infatuation for him. It became very evident to others that she was lost in something day and night. Something was killing her inside. She was not becoming possessive, but she was curious to know about everything he did—what time he reached for work, who were the people he met, and so on and so forth. That was the first time she was experiencing the feeling of love. As soon as her work got over, her first thought was to meet Victor. A few months later, after going through lots of emotional turmoil, she thought enough was enough—let me muster courage and tell him.

The following morning, she went to a public booth and dialled Victor's number. When Victor answered the phone, she uttered everything she had to say and went silent. She was expecting some response from Victor but was shocked to hear Victor hanging the phone up.

That night, Irene was not able to sleep. She desperately wanted to talk to Victor to see his expression. The following morning, unable to control her emotional thoughts, she dashed off the bed, got ready in no time, caught the bus, and reached the place where Victor was working as an apprentice.

After the security guards informed Victor that he had a visitor, he came out. At the first glance at Irene, he wanted to turn back and leave. But Irene's persistence to just have a few words made him to stay. He did not utter a single word but only listened to what Irene was saying. His silence was bothering her a lot. In the end, she told him, 'If you don't like me, at least don't ruin our friendship.'

Victor nodded and asked her to meet him in the evening at the same place where they had earlier met. Irene was relieved, finally. Whether he liked her not, she did not want to lose his friendship at any cost. Also in the back of her mind, she had hopes of winning him back. She thought that maybe he needed more time to think over the matter. And being friends with him would give her time to be with him and also to win him over.

Buoyed by this fresh thought, Irene started getting ready to meet Victor. Looking at the mirror, she made sure she did everything to look attractive. She reached the coffee place and saw Victor already waiting for her. There was a little feeling of uneasiness between them. But that faded away once Henrita arrived.

Victor stood and greeted her. They were very excited to see each other and forgot the fact that there was another person sitting with them. Henrita's eyes moved towards Irene. A gentle smile came upon Irene's face. Irene thought she had seen Henrita somewhere. She was not able to recollect when and where they had met, until Victor's introduction of her as their senior ignited a spark of memory. She had seen Henrita on the first day of college, during the dean's lecture session. She was in fact standing next to

Victor for some time that day, before she joined other passing-out seniors.

Slight uneasiness and a feeling of pain started to creep into Irene's heart. Irene had a smiling face on, trying hard to look cool, but she was beginning to feel that something was about to go wrong. After a while, Victor and Henrita got up and started to walk. Seeing them walk away, Irene got message. She felt a deep, piercing pain as if someone had shot an arrow into her heart. Tears started to flow down her cheeks, and she kept walking fast.

Once she reached her house, she immediately rushed to the bathroom to clean her face. There she burst into tears. After being there for a few minutes, until she felt she could handle the situation, she came out and started mingling with her friends. She behaved as if nothing had happened. With each passing day, she was trying hard to return to her normal self.

But deep inside her heart, the pain was tearing her apart. Sometimes she would get lost for hours while working on her assignments. She was craving a lot for Victor. She knew that now it was not possible to get Victor back, but she was expecting for some kind of miracle to bring him back. She resorted to reading the scriptures, which gave her mental peace. Whenever she went to church, her only wish from God was to bring her Victor back to him. This continued for several months, and when she found that nothing was working, she gradually slipped into a state of depression. Now she was feeling very lonely. Even when she tried hard to sleep after her working hours, her pain never allowed her to sleep peacefully. She liked sitting idle, and whenever she thought of Victor, her heart pained and tears came rolling down her cheeks. A few questions always rattled her mind—why doesn't Victor like me? Is there something wrong with me? Why do I have to undergo this pain?

Time went by, and the day came when all of them had to leave the college. It was graduation day. Irene didn't feel like attending the college. She met the dean and asked for a special permission to let someone else collect her certificate. She pretended that someone in her family was not well and hence would not be able to attend the graduation ceremony. The next day, Irene packed her luggage and boarded the bus to her parents' house. Her parents were very happy to see her but found that something was amiss. They did not ask her then, feeling she might be tired. But over a period of time, they noticed that Irene would lock herself in a room for several hours. They had no idea what was going on inside her mind. She was half dead. He brain had stopped working. She came out of the room only for eating lunch/dinner, after which, she again went back to her room. Initially, they thought she must be busy with her painting, or planning for her future, to start something of her own.

Now Irene's close companions were her room and her painful thoughts. Sometimes she would go for a walk. Spending time with nature was her favourite pastime from childhood—and now a pain reliever for her. She felt better when she spent time with nature. During one of the strolls, she happened to land at a book club. She had not seen a book club of this kind when she was a child. She saw people reading and borrowing books. Outside the book club, on the name board was written Mr and Mrs Derreck Book Club. 'All book lovers are invited' was encrypted below the board. Mr and Mrs Derreck, in their late seventies, had opened the book club a few months back. They wanted to do something with their savings, which was getting rusted, lying idle in the bank. Since both were fond of reading books, the idea of starting a book club came through. And within three months of its existence, it started attracting a good number of patrons.

Irene thought of giving the book club a dekko. Anyway, it wouldn't cause her any harm if she took more time than usual to get back home. She saw some people reading eagerly by the table, some skimming through books by the shelf, and some borrowing books to read at home at the counter. Irene strolled around the club, and her eyes zeroed in on a book that was related to healing pains. She picked the book from the shelf, pulled the chair, and started going through the pages. Initially, she felt bored, but as she started spending more time, her inner voice told her to explore more books on the same topic.

The next day, she came directly to the book club and picked two to three books and started reading. The topics discussed were a little heavy, but they were able to get her attention. To understand difficult topics requires a complete absorption of self. And now Irene was in a mental state where she was keen to know more about why she was undergoing the suffering, and that hooked her to the chapters. This continued for a month, and then beginning of the next month, as she got bored with philosophies, she thought of exploring history. Slowly, as the days went by, she was able to take control of herself. Now the pain was replaced by extensive knowledge of self, and now she wanted to read on different subjects. Also, this newfound habit kept her occupied, leaving her with no time to think of the past. Her topics ranged from history to mythology to science, both fiction and nonfiction.

As Irene got absorbed in reading books to get rid of her pain, a strange development was occurring in her, about which she was not aware. Her concentration powers were increasing. After a few months of continuous reading, she was able to finish three to four books in a day. She was able to read on any subject for hours, without getting the slightest bit bored. One day, while she was reading a book, she lifted her hand as usual to turn the page, but she encountered a strange thing. The page turned on its own. Surprised by this, she thought of moving another page—it turned too, without she having to flip it with her hand.

She was shocked by this incident. She had heard about mental power, but experiencing the same was incredible. She was now witnessing it herself. To remove her disbelief, she thought of trying something different. Instead of turning pages, she tried to move a book on the table.

Within moments of her looking at the book, it started to move towards the intended place. There was no doubt now. She found that she had an unusually high power of concentration. She could move things with her thoughts.

# PART 2

PART 2

# CHAPTER 7

After reaching home, Irene felt very tired, maybe because of excessive mental drain. She entered her room, locked the door, and slept for some time. After a few hours, when she woke up, it was almost evening. She noticed that something was happening to her. After the sleep, she felt very energetic, a sudden gush of positivity, as if someone injected a feel-good steroid in her. The pain which engulfed her for the last five months was slowly fading away. Initially, the mere thought of Victor would give her lots of pain, but now, she was able to feel good when she thought of him.

Her eyes moved towards her canvas. The object on it was half drawn. She thought of completing it and got up to take the brush. As she approached the brush, it started moving in air. She pinched herself to wake her up from the dream. But it was not a dream—it was reality. She looked at the canvas—it also started shaking. 'Is it an earthquake or what? What the hell is happening to me?' she wondered. Then her mind drifted to the incident that happened at the book club. She realised that she had acquired tremendous concentration power in the book club. Perhaps, the pain she suffered and while trying to rid her of the pain, letting herself be absorbed deeply to a thing she liked a lot and later scaling up to do more tasks in a limited time must have helped her to achieve this superhuman gift. A few months back, she was a powerless, directionless, and broken person. But now she was able to think clearly.

She took out a small note book and started to write. 'Whatever happens in the circle of Life, it happens for a reason. Just flow with whatever you are encountering and wait patiently till you acquire more power to overcome the grief.'

After placing the notebook back in her shelf, she wanted to understand and address how to channelise this psychic power. When she wanted to take a brush to paint, it started to fly, whereas she was able to comfortably pull out the notebook from the shelf, write in it, and put it back on the shelf. Her eyes again drifted towards the book. She kept staring at it for few minutes. It started to shake, and now she wanted that book to come to her. When that intention was conveyed through her thoughts, the book flew towards her. 'Bingo!' she thought. She kept practicing the same principle on the brush also. It also gave in to her intention. Buoyed by this fresh hidden gift, she came out of the room, looked at her mom and told her if she could serve her dinner now. She was feeling damn hungry.

Her mother felt nice that after a long hibernation, she had got her daughter back. Irene pulled up the dining chair and waited for her mom to serve dinner. Meanwhile, her eyes zeroed in on the spoon kept on the table. Very carefully, first ensuring that no one was looking at her and her mother was still in the kitchen, she started focusing on the spoon. The spoon started to bend, and she was able to do it with less mental force than necessary.

She had come across articles in papers on people who were capable of bending spoons. Well-known psychics like Yuri Geller and others used to bend spoon with the help of their psychic powers, and they had made lots of fame and money for themselves. But she was not very keen to follow them. She thought of doing something different.

She wanted to help people with her unique gift. That would be her main purpose for the rest of her life. But she had no idea about what to do. No matter how long it took, she was determined to find that one thing she would be able to help by her gift. She did not want people to believe that she was also one of the illusionists who used some kind of tricks to earn a livelihood. She wanted people to respect her and believe her that we all possessed some kind of gift in ourselves, and our main job was to find those gifts and utilise it to help people. And during this process, if you are rewarded financially, then that is the right way to live your life.

The difference between the old and the new Irene was that the latter was able to think clearly. If she was not doing anything beyond her limitations, she felt like she was exploding from within. Hence she wanted to take up a task that would match her mental alertness.

# CHAPTER 8

Days went by, thinking what needs to be done. Even though she liked painting a lot, before entering into making money from her paintings, which at this point of time she could have easily made, she was keen to explore more of her. If she failed in her mission, she could always come back to her passion. But her motto was to help people with this gift.

Sitting by the window and gazing at the sky for a long time, she did not notice when her mother came and placed her breakfast on the table, along with the morning newspaper. Irene hated reading papers as it only had news on burglary or the nation undergoing recession or some businessman launching a new service and expanding his business or some gossip on celebrities.

But this time she felt like going through the paper. As she was drinking her tea, Irene glanced at the pages one by one. In one of the pages at the bottom, she saw a headline that hooked her.

'City's seniors conned by men disguising as loan agents, who promised to loan them money at very low interest rates'

The task of getting the culprit behind the bars, she thought, would be her first mission to test her innate abilities. And as per the news, this was a perennial problem harassing most of the elderly gentlemen. And the police were not able to catch them because they could not track calls made from their cell phones. It was a big racket, and lots of people were involved. Once the job was over, they discarded their old SIM card and operated with a new one, that is, a new cell connection, and proceeded to hunt down their new target. Bradley police used their sources to come out with the sketches of these people as narrated by the elderly people. But every time, a different person would pose as the loan agent.

This meant that the loan agents disguised themselves properly before approaching the seniors, so that no one would be able to recognise them.

# CHAPTER 9

The next day morning, Irene went to meet the police handling this case. From the newspaper, she was not able to get any details of the senior citizens. At least by getting hold of the concerned authority, she would get the address of the people who were conned.

Bradley Police Headquarters

Irene at the police helpdesk: May I see the police officer in charge of handling the case of duping the senior citizens? The article appeared in yesterday's newspaper.

Helpdesk to Irene: You may please meet Officer Victor who is sitting next to the discussion room—straight from here and then turn left.

Irene: Thank you!

Irene to Victor: Hello, officer, I am Irene. I happened to read the article which appeared in yesterday's city newspaper about the elderly citizens getting conned by alleged loan agents. I wanted to know if you can help me with the details of the senior citizens. I am asking the details because my parents are also seniors, and I don't want them to go through this ordeal. If you may please help, that would be great.

Victor to Irene: That's really thoughtful of you, Ms Irene! We want people to come forward and get educated themselves so that they can avert these kinds of incidents. Also, please take my card—if there are any issues, you can call me on this number.

On leaving the police headquarters, Irene had a smile on her face. It was not because she was able to get the details she intended, but because of the name Victor. When she heard the name Victor from the police helpdesk, her mind took her back to her college days, but this time she did not feel any pain. A police officer with a similar name only reinforced her belief that the pain she encountered was for some reason. Had she not gone through the rough patch in her life, she would not have found her purpose. She thanked God—for whatever he had bestowed on her. Now she didn't feel a craving for victor, and neither did she feel like hating him. Had she not fallen in love with him, she would not have been the special person that she is now. So she is thankful to him that he came into her life.

# CHAPTER 10

S ector 203

Most of the elderly people who got conned had their residential address in sector 203. She entered the block, turned left, and pulled her car over. The first house was that of Mr Darius. From the police headquarters, she had got the information that Darius's family was the first one to get conned by the fraudsters. Mr Darius was a retired teacher, and from whatever little savings he had, he purchased a house in this sector. The house was not big from enough for him and his wife. They had one daughter, who was settled in France. So in a way, they were staying alone. In order to get rid of boredom, they thought of starting something which required huge capital. Even if they mortgaged their home and added a little bit of savings, they would not able to fund the venture for more than a year. And that is a bad business idea. For any new venture, there should be enough money to support it financially for at least three years, till it shows profit. With that intention, they approached banks but had to face rejection as they did not have a strong collateral to support.

She heard the same kind of story from all the fourteen seniors who were duped. She came back home and called Victor and asked him if he could meet him tomorrow morning at 10 a.m. at the police headquarters. She had some information that needed to be shared.

# CHAPTER 11

**Irene to Victor**: As per my meetings with all the citizens, I am able to understand their modus operandi. I thought I will share that with you. This is how they work.

Someone from the bank gives the data of rejected loan cases to the fraudsters. And these people target those rejected cases by offering them more money at less interest rates. The only condition they put forward is that the senior citizens need to shell out a little money from their pockets initially so that they can bribe the bank officers and clear their loan papers. Only once the loan is sanctioned, would they charge their commission, which is hardly anything. And the initial money which they would spend would not go waste—it would be converted to shares and those shares can be sold whenever they want and get the money refunded. And these fraudsters promise to arrange money from private finance companies and not from any legal government institutions or banks. The promise of refunding their initial money in the form of shares acts as a trap, and all the senior citizens fall for this trap.

One more thing I noticed was that there was a pattern. These guys ask small amounts initially and then gradually increase to large amounts. When they feel that the target cannot afford to pay now, they disconnect all connections with them and just vanish.

But there is one catch in that—not all seniors were conned. As per my conversation with Mr Jeff, another senior citizen, he had a requirement. He went through the same process, and his loan was sanctioned. It is highly likely that these guys targeted Mr Jeff first, got his loan done, and then approached others, quoting his example.

This made others to believe them and by that time they wait patiently to get their loan money, all of them vanished taking whatever they got from these seniors. It is huge money they got away with combining all of them.

**Victor to Irene:** Even we thought of backtracking Jeff's loan details when he started staying paying them back and we did also. But unfortunately Jeff's son gave him the remaining money, and he closed the loan amount one week before they all vanished away. When we reached the place mentioned by Jeff, where he used to deliver the monthly instalment cheques, we saw the place locked and on the outside was mentioned 'For Sale'. When we enquired with the owner of the plot, he said a few people had taken the place from him for a lease for six months. When we verified all the documents submitted to the owner at the time of lease by these people, they proved to be forged. So there was hardly anything we could do.

**Irene to Victor:** Now to catch them, what I feel is, I need to set up a trap so that they approach me. For that, I would require your help. I will let you know.

**Victor to Irene:** Sure! I am always there.

# CHAPTER 12

I rene, with the help of Victor, was able to identify one apartment in Block 203 that had a lawn attached to it. Victor spoke to the owner of the house and arranged to get it for a very minimal rate. She invested whatever she had received during her apprenticeship days towards the apartment rent. The apartment was leased on her name for a period of six months. She approached her father and asked for some amount as a loan to pursue her painting career. She thought of holding her own painting exhibition.

Irene shifted her base to Block 203. She started painting. She started displaying all the finished stuff on the lawn with a minimal price attached to it so that buyer, if he or she liked the painting, should not think twice about buying it.

As the days passed by, visitors started flocking to her lawn. Hers was the only home with painting displayed, and these attracted passersby who came to at least have a look. Her painting started selling. Initially, it was one or two paintings in a day, but then after a month, because of word of mouth, it increased to ten to twelve pieces per day. She drew her paintings targeting adults and children in mind. Generally, once children like something, they will pester their parents to buy it.

Some of the parents also approached her, requesting her to teach their kids how to paint. Irene thought that was a good way of earning additional income and getting more publicity. She agreed for the same, and during the weekends, she taught children in the mornings. This reminded her of childhood days when she used teach at the tuition centre.

A few months later, the number of children grew; also her paintings started to get more patrons. Now she thought this was the correct time to approach banks for loans. She, with the help of Victor, listed down the names of all the nearby banks to be approached for getting loans. Her objective was to get a loan to open up a mini painting museum and learning centre for children. She now had enough patrons and credibility in Block 203 that getting a reference for bank verification purpose was very easy.

She approached all the banks they had planned. Submitted all the documents which included her source of income and working as a entrepreneur and aspiring to open up a mini painting museum and learning centre. The capital required for opening and running it was so huge, she knew the bank would definitely not approve it.

As expected, she started getting calls from the bank that they were going through her papers, and that as soon as there was some headway, they would let her know. After a week's time, when there was no response, she approached all the banks personally. She was told that her income was not sufficient to get the amount she was requesting. Hence it was rejected.

After her case was rejected by all the banks, she was now waiting for the call from the people for whom she had laid the trap. One afternoon, as she was packing her painting to be handed over to the customer, she received a call from a private finance company. She was told that if there was any requirement for a loan, whether it was secured or unsecured, they could help her get that from a private finance. 'If you are interested, we can come and collect the documents from you to take it ahead,' they said.

Irene was at last having her last laugh. She informed Victor about it and asked him to be present when they came to collect the document. Next day, a person came, dressed in formal attire. He was looking as if he worked for some sales company. He introduced himself, handed over his card, took the documents, and left. Irene felt nothing suspicious. The person asked neither for some early deposit nor for some kind of pre-hand payment. Generally, that was the pattern she had observed in the previous con cases.

**Irene to Victor**: Hi Victor, have they changed the modus operandi? What do you think?

**Victor to Irene**: Let's wait till his response. Anyway, he has taken the document.

The following day, Irene received a call from the sales agent. In an apologetic tone, he confessed he was not able to convince his superiors to grant her loan and that he was sorry to inform her that her loan had been rejected. Irene informed Victor about the same. It was not going anywhere. Their case had been rejected by most of the banks, but still they had not been approached by the people whom they were looking for.

Immediately, an idea struck Irene. He called up Victor and requested his help to use his contacts to get the idea executed. She told Victor, 'Don't worry about money. I am earning well now. I can take some risk. Ask them how much they will charge for getting this stuff done.'

# CHAPTER 13

The next day in *Daily News*, at the bottom of the first page, an article was published, whose headline read thus: 'Painting by Irene picked for $50,000 at Block 203'

Irene called up Victor and thanked him. 'Nice ad, buddy.' She then added, 'I have a gut feeling, I might get a call by today afternoon or tomorrow morning.'

Her gut feeling was right. Since morning she started getting calls from the media to know more about her so that they can fill their pages with stories about the upcoming painter. In the afternoon, while she was taking rest after dealing with the media guys, by telling them cooked-up stories, her phone rang. The person on the other side introduced himself as one of the sales agents of a private finance company. And he asked Irene if she needed a loan.

Irene to sales agent: Yes, I do have a requirement, but my case got rejected by all major banks, and now I have lost hope.

Sales agent to Irene: What is the purpose of the loan?

Irene to sales agent: I am planning to start my own mini museum and learning centre for children. And that would require huge amount of capital.

Sales agent: Hmm, correct. If you don't mind, may I pay a visit to your house, and then we can discuss more on how we can work together to achieve your objective. May be tomorrow at 12 noon, if you are fine with that?

Irene to sales agent: Sure, not an issue. What documents would you like to see?

Sales agent: Nothing much, just the usual documents the banks ask for. We take up those cases which gets rejected by the banks.

And we have a success rate of almost 100 per cent.

Irene: Wow, that's cool. I have blocked my time for you for tomorrow.

Sales agent: Thank you and have a nice day!

Irene: You too!

Irene was excited but was not sure if he was one of them. Earlier they had similar ones where the person seems to be fake one but in the end he came out to be from a genuine finance company. The problem in this field is that there are two kinds of people: the first kind who take money and get the work done, and the second, those who take money and run away. It is the latter kind she would like to track. However, this time she did not want to inform Victor until and unless she was doubly sure.

The following day, Irene was eagerly waiting to see that person, but even after clock showed 12.30, there was no sign of him. Dejected, she thought he may not appear. She turned back and saw a person walking towards her. He reached the lawn and waved his hand at Irene to open the gate.

# CHAPTER 14

Expecting his arrival, Irene had already arranged the chair and table on the lawn.

Sales agent: Hi! My name is Wilson. I am part of Barclays Financials. I am sorry I am a little late. I got lost on my way while looking for your house.

Irene: That's fine, Mr Wilson. Here are the documents which you were expecting.

Wilson: How much loan are you planning to apply for?

Irene: I will need capital of up to $2,000,00. It will take care of my operational expenses.

Wilson: Hmmmm.

(He started going through documents. He took out his cell phone and dialled a number. He spoke for a few minutes and then turned towards Irene.)

Wilson: I went through your documents, and it is perfect. In fact, I was on other line with my colleague who takes care of verification and other things. He would like to have a word with you. Along with these documents, we would be charging our processing fees of $500.

Irene: That's OK. Processing fees are normal.

(Wilson handed over the phone to Irene, and she started chatting with his colleague.)

Sales agent to Irene: Good afternoon, madam. Thank you for giving us an opportunity to take care of your loan requirements. We will definitely serve you as best as possible. Wilson tells me that your documents are perfect, and there would not be any problem. But I would like to make something clear to you before we process your documents. We are the official partners of a private finance company. We take up only rejected cases and help people who need finance immediately with less interest. For the same, we offer customer shares of those private companies, which is usually 15–16 per cent of your total loan amount. Once your loan amount is disbursed, you can refund your shares certificate in the market and whatever value the private company is holding on that day, you would get the same rate. In a way, if you see, there is a high chance of getting more refund money. Generally, our disbursal takes twenty-five to thirty days, and by that time, shares of the company usually jump from their normal value. If you are fine with this arrangement, then you can hand over the money, 16 per cent, that is, $32,000, to Mr Wilson in a day's time. And he would hand over to you the share certificates and the loan agreement, and then we can start the disbursal process.

Irene to sales agent: Thank you for your information! I will take it ahead with Mr Wilson.

Irene then cut the call.

Irene to Wilson: This is a unique way of processing a loan I guess. Generally banks don't take money upfront except for some documental charges.

Wilson: Yes, Irene. You are right. That's why they charge huge interest rates also. In our case, once you buy the shares of the private company, you become part of the conglomerate, and in case, in future, if you need a loan top-up, you just have to produce those share certificates along with the loan agreement. They would disburse the money with the same interest rates. In case of banks, they charge huge interest rates even if you want a top-up.

Irene: What are your credentials? How can I trust you?

Wilson: We keep our customer's name confidential. There are many in Block 203 who have taken loan from us. Since you insist on knowing my credentials, I will share the name of one person, Mr Jeff, who stays right across that block. You can check with him.

Irene: OK, fine. But arranging such a huge amount of money will take some time. I will at least need two days' time.

Wilson: Never mind. I will contact you in two days' time. Thank you for your time.

As soon as the sales agent left, Irene calls up Victor and shares all this information. Victor asks her if she could share his contact number so that he could track her and, without wasting time, get hold of him. But Irene recalled that the sales agent had used his cell phone, which he handed over to her for her to speak to another agent. So there was no way she could get his cell number. 'He did call me on my cell, but I think it was from a public booth,' Irene said.

Victor exclaimed, 'Oh oh, very smart! However, we will catch him. Let him come after two days. I will be with you. Thanks, Irene.'

# CHAPTER 15

There was something going on in Wilson's mind. The meeting did not go as per his expectation. He was sure that if Irene has asked for two days to lend the money, it means either she would be planning to shift her money to her bank or she is buying time to get some help. In either of the case, his plan of taking control of the $50,000 was not working out.

Instead of waiting for two days, he decides to execute his plan that very same night. Robbing this amount would help him keep going for a few months till he gets his next target. With this intention, he took out his cell, dialled one number, and spoke to him at length. Within the next fifteen minutes, he was on the go. He reached Block 203 at 11 p.m. He waited till the neighbours turned off their lights.

Irene was busy cleaning utensils. She was not able to hear the sound of the windows creaking. She went to the dining table and started to have her dinner. She felt some shadows approaching her from behind. When she turned left, nothing was there. As she regained her posture, suddenly an arm dragged her neck from behind.

Not able to breathe, she hit the chair with her legs and moved back with the man grabbing her from behind. With her left arm, she got hold of his mask, and with her right elbow, she gave him a nice punch. She hit him hard, and he moved away from her. As he moved away, the mask, which was being held by her left hand, came off his head.

Irene was shocked to see Wilson at this point of time. She was expecting him only after two days, and moreover, she had not had observed any killing in the previous con cases. As Irene was thinking, Wilson from his left took out small pistol and from his right silencer so that no one could hear the sound.

Irene was standing at point blank distance from Wilson. She had controlled metals, but she had never practiced her mental powers on humans, and this was not the correct time for experiment. Whatever she was good at, she needed to do that. Behind her, at a comfortable distance, were knifes hanging in the kitchen.

As Wilson was gradually fitting the silencer to the piston, with a smirk on his face, Irene started to stare at the knife. Wilson thought it would be too late by the time she got those knifes to defend her. He looked down to refit the pistol to the silencer properly. As he looked up, he saw one knife at a scorching pace entering his left thigh.

As he was trying to understand what was going on, he saw two knifes flying simultaneously towards him and hitting him in his right thigh and the shoulder holding the pistol. As he looked towards Irene, he realised that he was not in front of an ordinary human; a feeling of shock and awe pierced his heart. He did not feel like giving up. He slowly tried to raise his hand to aim at Irene.

The last knife in the kitchen flew towards Wilson with the intent of cutting his wrist. The knife cut the wrist, blood oozed from the wound, and the impact made Wilson to pull the trigger. The bullet hit the kitchen windows, and in the living room lay Wilson in a pool of blood.

Irene called up Victor, and within a fraction of time, Victor arrived with his team and ambulance. Both were rushed to the hospital. Irene narrated the incident, but she did not reveal anything about her mental skills. She told that when Wilson shot her, she managed to dodge the bullet, and it hit the window. To defend herself, she threw knifes on him which got him injured. Her statement was recorded, and Victor did not charge any case on her as it was completely an act of self-defense.

In the other room, the doctor was trying to save Wilson, who had lost immense blood. He was kept in Intensive Care Unit under strict observation. While Victor was waiting outside to have a word with the doctor, a packet was handed over to him by the nurse. She told it was found in his coat. The packet contained a few papers and one cell phone. He switched on the mobile phone and went on to check his last few dialled numbers.

He was shocked when he saw the number of a known person from Block 203.

Irene still resides in Block 203. She was honoured for her bravery by the mayor of the city. She was also granted a land to open a mini museum and learning centre. All the cost was partly borne by the people and partly funded by the mayor's influential friends.

She still helps people with her skills. Whenever she gets some interesting case, she calls up Victor and gets her adrenaline rolling.

Jeff was arrested as he acted as an accomplice to the crime. Wilson used to share a small percentage of the amount with Jeff for supporting him.

Irene included a few more learnings in her diary. She consolidated all the learnings and ensured that it was put up on the walls of the museum and the learning centre.

Learnings on the Wall

Whatever happens in the circle of life, it happens for a reason. Just flow with whatever you are encountering and wait patiently till you acquire more power to overcome the grief.

Everyone should strive towards identifying their gifts.

Once you identify that gift, sustain it and utilise it for serving the human race. In the process, you will be rewarded. And that is the true way of living life.

# ABOUT THE AUTHOR

Award-winning author Rajith Rajappan overcame several early obstacles in life—from an impoverished childhood to learning difficulties—to become a successful professional. A lifelong student of self-improvement, his first book *The Illuminator—Access to Universal Intelligence*, released in 2011, went on to win many awards in the United States in 2012 (more details could be found in www.sbpra.com/RajithRajappan).

He is an optimistic person, who seems ever enthusiastic about life and living. His role in life is to inspire and motivate and to raise the spirits of those around him.

*Irene and Her Sixth Sense* is his second book in the offing. He can be reached at rajith.rajappan@gmail.com